WHO

GIVES

A FICO

By

LAWRENCE MARTIN

LEGAL DISCLAIMER

Table of Contents

INTRODUCTION

"Money never made a man happy yet, nor will it. There is nothing in its nature to produce happiness. The more a man has, the more he wants. Instead of filling a vacuum, it makes one."

--Benjamin Franklin

My first encounter with credit

Welcome to the real world where everything you do involves someone pulling your credit report, whether you are buying a home, applying for a job, getting an education or even purchasing a cell phone.

My story with credit starts at the age of 19 stepping into, what my parents would call, the real world. Where, if you don't make it happen, things will just happen to you (victim of circumstance). It was my time to grind and become self-sufficient, no more allowances or free lunches (East Park). In my mind, it was me against the world and my perception of life was more fantasy, guarded by theory without experience.

At this time, I was a Student-Athlete playing on the Men's Basketball team at Mississippi Gulf Coast Community

College in Perkingston, MS, with no real goals or a clearly defined vision. I just went with the flow of life, until the flow stopped, and it was time to make big boy decisions. So, what's next? What is my next move? Where do I go from here? Well, long story short:

I ended up in Orlando, Florida. I say I ended up because there was no plan to stay. Again, life was happening to me, but I was cool with it. Orlando was a fresh start. Plus, I had the opportunity to be around family, meet new people and watch the city beautiful unfold. There was one problem, you need a car to live in Orlando, no exceptions because the bus thing is not an option. Trust me, it's too hot to wait for a bus. The sun will constantly remind you of that; you need a car with a functional A/C unit.

After working a few months, I decided to go to a local used car dealership; you know, the buy-here-pay-here kind, just to get an idea of where I stood in the car qualification category. Maybe, just maybe, I could get a loan as a means of purchasing a vehicle. I looked at a few cars and became really eager to drive anything rolling, almost desperate. The car salesman pulled me into his tiny corner office filled with paperwork everywhere with the world's oldest, dustiest computer, asking for my social security number. Within minutes of pulling my credit, he looked at me and said, "You have no credit." This was not a shock to me, totally understandable, but what he said afterward kind of threw me off. He looked me square in the eyes like it was time for straight talk and said, "No credit is worse than bad credit, my friend." What a profound concept.

No credit is worse than bad credit. At this time, I didn't know what a credit score was, how to build credit or where to start. No one was teaching credit or finances from that perspective. Or maybe, at that age, I didn't hear anything about it. This was my first reality check on how the world of credit worked.

For the record, my parents gave me their 1985 Cadillac Fleetwood. Of course, I slapped tint on it, threw a little sound in it and I was rolling. Just so you know.

Now that we've got a ride, it's time to look for a place to stay. You want to be a big boy, you gotta play by the rules. I had plans to make moves to get into my first apartment, and, of course, split the rent with my brother. Well, we filled out a few applications, and as Suze Orman would say, "Denied, denied, denied." Now think about this for a moment, where you stay can have a powerful influence on your quality of life, so choose wisely.

After being denied due to having no established credit, we eventually found a place that welcomed us with open arms. As I remember the office manager was a sweet

Hispanic lady saying, "Come, you don't need nothing, nothing, nothing. Except for a huge deposit with first and last month's rent." I loved it! We were in the game!

In my adult life, no one - and I mean no one - has ever asked to see my college degree or my G.P.A. However, I have had my credit pulled for everything from rental cars, auto loans, credit cards, jobs, mortgages, car insurance, home insurance, life insurance, utilities, cell phones, and in my Shirley Caesar voice, "You name it!" My point is this: just take a look at how much of our everyday life is touched by credit in some way.

Even if you get sick and accrue medical bills, watch what happens if you do not pay them in a timely manner. You will have a big surprise waiting for you on your next visit to the car dealership. Oh, speaking of medical debt, it is the number one reason most Americans file for bankruptcy.

Now, I must insert this disclaimer; I do not condone nor support certain types of debt. It's all about the R.O.I (Return on Investment). If it doesn't make dollars, it doesn't make sense. The student loan crisis is not a crisis because of the loan. Tell that to the lawyer making six figures a month. It's a crisis because of the lack of income. It's just that simple.

In the real world, if you are not actively involved with your credit, whether you like it or not, you will be penalized for it. You will pay the price for bad credit. Cash is King, but Credit runs the Kingdom! Now, don't try to steal my quote. You heard it here first.

Eventually, I established my credit through a few credit cards and a car loan. Life was good. I had a $16,000 credit card from Bank of America with four other high limit cards that I had maxed out; you couldn't tell me anything. But when it rains, it pours. When the floods come, you better be prepared.

Cash flow was steady until I lost my job for a few months. I decided not to make payments (big mistake) and then the phone started to ring like crazy. The interest rates began to double, and before I knew it, I was in a deep hole.

Now, this was an eye-opening experience for me because, before then, I had impeccable credit and never missed a payment in my life, period. I learned how to negotiate and settle a debt with the big banks. I also learned a valuable lesson about the aftermath of taxes when you decide to settle the debt for a lesser amount. I worked my fingers to the bone to clear this debt and I'm proud to say we cleared $60,000 worth of debt in four years. Give it up!

However, had I known what I'm going to teach you in this book, there was a better way to deal with debt and credit. I learned about budgeting and writing out a plan, but I quickly found out that understanding your consumer rights is also a powerful tool, as it relates to financial literacy.

My wife, Rhonda, and I got married on June 19th, 2004. In less than a year, we bought our first home and had our first baby girl, Laniah. All I can say is my life has never been the same. Then Lawrence Jr. came, and we soon became crowded in our lovely 3-bedroom 1-bath starter home, and we all felt it. Now, it's time to look for a bigger place; now it's time to check the credit.

After paying back all of our outstanding debt, I was happy to shout the Debt Free scream, minus the mortgage. However, there was something else I noticed: my bills were paid, but my credit score was still stuck. At first, I thought eventually it would go up on its own.

It never did! After going through the experience of paying back all those credit cards, why would I go and get another one? How could I put myself in that type of hardship again? So, I decided to wait a few years before I reestablished my credit. That was reality check number two. If you are not actively involved with your credit, your scores will stay in the same place.

In this book, you will learn the secrets of the FICO score. How to use the scores to your advantage and the five key components that make up the FICO score. My objective is to make sure consumers are fully aware of how to maximize their scores and that they do not fall victim to life happening to them.

Your credit score is one of the most critical factors in your financial life. It determines if you will be approved for a loan or line of credit. A credit score is a mathematically calculated number developed by the Fair Isaac Corporation (FICO) that lenders use to rate potential customers when determining the likelihood that a consumer will pay their bills on time.

A credit score, or credit rating, is determined by using five main criteria as defined by MyFico.com: your payment history, which accounts for 35 percent of your credit score; the amounts owed, or utilization, which accounts for 30 percent of your credit score; the length of your credit history, which accounts for 15 percent of your credit score; new credit, which accounts for 10 percent of your credit score, and the types of credit used. which accounts for 10 percent of your credit score.

Let's start with payment history. Payment history shows the history of how you paid your bills, either on-time or late, but unfortunately, it does not show if your bills were paid before the due date. Amounts owed shows the total amount of credit you have available. If your balance is near the credit limit, this may lower your credit score. The length of history indicates how long you have had credit.

If your credit history is 2-years-old or less, you should not be surprised if your scores are low. New credit indicates how many times you have applied for new credit. If you open too many new accounts in a short period of time, this may lower your credit score.

The types of credit used indicates the types of accounts you have, such as revolving or installment accounts. Revolving accounts are usually credit cards. Installmentaccounts are usually mortgages, auto loans, etc.

The FICO credit score model ranges from 300-850, with 850 being an excellent score and 300 being the worst score. The higher the credit score, the lower the interest rate you will receive for a loan or line of credit.

Having a good credit score can save you thousands of dollars in interest over the life of a loan or line of credit. A good credit score is generally in the range of 680-740, but may vary from lender to lender.

Chapter 1

THE HISTORY OF THE FAIR ISAAC CORPORATION (FICO)

"If money is your hope for independence you will never have it. The only real security that a man will have in this world is a reserve of knowledge, experience, and ability."

--Henry Ford

The circular flow of money in the environment is a very important aspect of our economy. The flow of money helps consumers exchange something of value, which results in business transactions. There are several ways in which money can circulate around the financial environment and one approach is through lending and borrowing.

Formal lending and borrowing can be traced back to Ancient Rome where "banking" was carried out by certain private individuals known as *Argentarii*, Greek money changers known as *Trapezites,* priests and other types of roman bankers. To fast forward everything, we now have modern and innovative methods, which lead to the birth of financial institutions.

Businesses play a vital role in our financial, marketing and economic environments. Management theories evolved through time to help businesses operate better and contribute more to society.

Decision-making is a crucial aspect in managing businesses, which is why people in the early corporate world used scientific approaches that resulted in different innovations.

In the 1950s, U.S. consumers avoided the financial markets due to the Great Depression in the 1930s. It was a cultural norm to pay cash or trade goods and services, but credit was a rare subject. You know, my great grandfather's number one rule in money was, *Pay cash* (Daddy Tome R.I.P).

In 1956, an engineer named Bill Fair and a mathematician named Earl Isaac met while working at Stanford Research Institute in California. The partnership of Bill Fair and Earl Isaac paved the way to FICO Incorporated, which stands for Fair Isaac Company. Fair and Isaac created a synthesis of mathematics and computers to help businesses make better decisions.

The company and its founders pioneered the use of credit scoring, which is enabled, through the use of algorithms, to predict the credit risk of a borrower. They offered to test it with several businesses who were lending to explain how credit scoring worked.

One of the companies responded, and in 1958, the first credit scoring system was built. From the 1960s to the 1970s, credit scoring became commercialized and helped with an analytical prediction for lenders.

This challenged the standard practices of lenders, and eventually changed, as well as some of their prejudicial ways since the system proved that race was not a basis of credit performance.

The credit scoring system gave an equal opportunity for people to borrow, resulting in the Distinctive Service Award, won by Fair and Isaac from the American Bankers Association.

In 1972, the company introduced another innovation, the first automated application processing system. The system was used to further help businesses and was applied to customer management. In 1986, the first automated credit account management system was created. It paved the way for the explosive use of credit cards in the years that followed. The system is known today as FICO Triad

Customer Manager, and it manages most of the world's credit card accounts.

In addition, to further increase the scope of their technology, FICO started to expand its operations and entered the market of Europe in the early 1980s. It was then followed by Asia Pacific countries such as Singapore, Australia, China, India, Japan, Malaysia, and Thailand. The company grew and reached Africa and the Middle East as well. Currently, the company is continuously expanding all over the globe. The innovated system of the company during the 1980s created an impact in lending decisions.

It was in 1989 that the first broad-based credit score was released, and in 1991 the company became available at all three major credit bureaus. FICO scores continue to be virtually synonymous with credit risk scores. The company did not stop aiming higher as they added two more innovations that transformed business decisions.

The FICO Falcon Fraud Manager was launched in 1992, it detects credit and fraud with the use of neural networks. Up to date, it is considered the most successful use of artificial intelligence that protects two-thirds of credit card transactions globally.

In 1995, Fannie Mae and Freddie Mac, a Federal Housing Finance Agency, recommended FICO scores in evaluating mortgage loans. Another key technology was introduced, the Decision Rules Management System. The award-winning and powerful FICO Blaze Advisor, a Decision Rules Management System, gave businesses flexibility and a fast way to govern rules behind business decisions.

In early 2000, consumers were able to buy Credit Scores with the launch of myFICO.com and newly introduced the FICO Score Open Access Program. Through this, banks give FICO scores to customers, which help millions of consumers in having a better way to manage their credit health.

At present, there are more than 10 Billion FICO scores sold each year. FICO scores of borrowers are used by lenders to assess whether credit will be extended or not, in conjunction with their credit reports and risks.

Nowadays, FICO scores consider different factors in five areas to determine creditworthiness; namely payment history, current level of indebtedness, types of credit used, length of credit history and new credit accounts.

FICO continues to grow and revolutionize in an exponential phase with new solutions, improving customer experience, fighting cybercrime, helping control fraud, security and more.

In 2015, the company launched FICO Analytic Cloud and FICO Decision Management Suite, democratizing the world of decision management and making the power of predictive analytics faster, easier and more cost-effective than ever before.

As FICO helps businesses and consumers make better decisions, their mission continues. This is just a brief history of the FICO score changing with the world in many ways.

Chapter 2

THE FICO SCORE AND HOW IT WORKS

Courage is being scared to death but saddling up anyway.

--John Wayne

Good credit is necessary in the United States today. There is a huge network of credit reporting agencies that keep track of the credit rating of the consumers. These agencies check the creditworthiness of a borrower every time they apply for a loan, credit card or any type of credit.

No credit is worse than bad credit; nevertheless, bad credit means big business to some companies. Different companies gain millions of dollars every year from people who lack awareness concerning their credit and FICO scores.

The good news is that your FICO score has a formula you can use to your utmost advantage. Before we proceed with how the FICO score works, we need to have a good understanding of the FICO score itself.

The FICO score was introduced in the previous chapter as a mathematical model that is used to assess the credit risk of a consumer. Through the use of FICO scores, businesses can make better decisions before lending, with lowered risk of having no money collected at all.

The FICO score depicts whether consumers are at risk of becoming 90 days late on an account within the next 24 months. The existence of FICO scores made thousands of lenders use them every day so they can accurately understand a consumer's credit risk, which results in well-informed credit-granting decisions.

FICO scores are the most widely used credit score in the country, with approximately 90 percent of lenders utilizing them. Since FICO scores became synonymous with the credit risk score, it is a number that predicts the likelihood of a consumer to pay their bills, credit obligations and how timely they make the payment.

The FICO scores are calculated from the data in a consumer's credit reports, which are sent to the three main credit bureaus; namely Equifax, TransUnion, and Experian. Every consumer has three FICO Scores, one for each of the three credit bureaus.

The scores consider information about payment, history, use of available credit and other factors. Most consumers have FICO scores for each of their credit reports since FICO calculates solely on information about credit reports that are maintained at the credit reporting agencies. If by any chance a consumer does not have any recent credit history reported, then there is no FICO score.

FICO scores are dynamic and can increase or decrease if and when the data in the credit bureau changes. Since credit agencies carry many types of information from a consumer's credit report, the information and the patterns in hundreds of thousands of past credit reports will be compared.

This allows FICO scores to estimate a person's level of future credit risk. It is calculated on a real-time basis and shows the current information at the time a consumer and lender would request for it. The scores generally range from 300; which is implied as poor, to 850; interpreted as perfect.

The higher the FICO score is, the lower the risk for the lender, which means better credit terms for consumers. Eventually, FICO scores are in the hands of borrowers for the reason that it is based on their credit habits as recorded in credit reports. Their credit reports with the bureau from which they want their score must contain enough recent information to base their credit score upon.

Why the FICO scores matter is an important question I want to answer in this reading. It is agreed upon that the scores do not determine whether a consumer is approved for a line of credit or the assigned interest rate since the decision is ultimately up to the lender.

The main point is that it helps the lender make a better credit approval decision, which leads us to focus on how consumers will be able to achieve that. The scores are very essential since FICO scores allow the lending process for a consumer to be faster and fairer. Moreover, it provides borrowers with more credit choices at competitive rates.

People can get faster answers from lenders since the scores streamline the application process. In addition, it applies the same set of standards to all borrowers. If the current scores from the credit reporting agencies are different, it is probably because the information those agencies have might be different from one another.

Each FICO score is based on information the credit bureau keeps on file about the consumer. However, if the information is identical at all three credit reporting agencies, each FICO score should be very close.

Finally, as borrowers prepare to apply for a loan, they have the opportunity to see what a lender sees, which is a credit history that is summarized, and all rolled up into a three-digit number.

Chapter 3

THE SCORE CALCULATION

Live as if you were to die tomorrow. Learn as if you were to live forever.

--Mahatma Gandhi

The Five Key Elements to the FICO Score

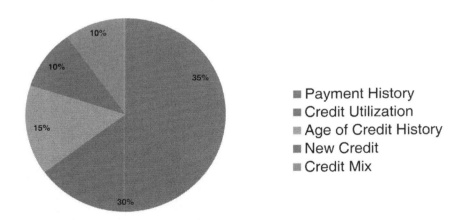

- Payment History
- Credit Utilization
- Age of Credit History
- New Credit
- Credit Mix

Score Range 300 – 850 = 550

The FICO Ratings

How do you rate your Credit?

Excellent Credit	750+
Good Credit	700-749
Fair Credit	650-699
Poor Credit	600-649
Bad Credit	Below 599

For a quick overview, FICO scores are calculated based on the categories presented above. The importance of any one factor in a borrower's credit calculation depends on the overall information in the credit report. Therefore, it is impossible to measure the exact impact of a single component in how the credit score is calculated.

The entire report should be considered. The levels of importance shown in the illustration above are FICO scores for the general population and vary for different credit profiles. This chapter will discuss the details regarding the elements, how scores are determined, or simply, how the FICO score works.

The previous chapter discussed how FICO scores help lenders answer important questions through a mathematical formula that makes the lending decisions faster, safer and fairer. It is also crucial for consumers to understand how their credit activities and behaviors are considered when calculating for FICO scores.

Scoring algorithms used in the calculation have been customized based on the type of loan. It is understandable how consumers can become confused by several scores and scoring models. The succeeding chapters will enlighten you on how the scoring model works. Different scoring models are needed and utilized by different companies. Before jumping into that section, we need to have an understanding of how the FICO scores work.

As mentioned before, FICO scores focus on five key predictive categories, also known as the "five key elements to the FICO score." It is basically the components of a credit score. The information gathered in a borrower's credit reports will be used by FICO and broken down into categories.

Each of the five elements holds different weights. It shows which among the components FICO scores give the most attention, as it will have a different percentage. Two of the categories contribute roughly two-thirds of a borrower's

FICO score. These five elements will be thoroughly discussed since is it important to how FICO Score is calculated.

The Five Key Elements to the FICO Score

1. Payment History	35%	193 points
2. Credit Utilization	30%	165 points
3. Age of Credit History	15%	83 points
4. New Credit	10%	55 points
5. Credit Mix	10%	55 points

As shown above, the first element on the list is **Payment History,** which makes up 35 percent of the total credit score. It is valued at 193 points once converted.

The second is **Credit Utilization,** which is 30 percent of the total credit score. If converted, it is equal to 165 points.

The third element is **Age of Credit History**, which makes up 15 percent of the total credit score. It is equal to 83 points after conversion. The last two elements are **New Credit** and **Credit Mix**; each comprises 10 percent of the total credit score. Both have a 55-point value if converted.

Payment History

The first category is the top-rated factor for the component of the scoring models. Lenders want to know the past and present history of a person. It shows if the borrower has missed payments, how often, how recently and how late they were. Making the repayment of a past debt is the most important factor in calculating credit scores. According to FICO, the past long-term behavior of a borrower is used to forecast future long-term behavior. This category can be broken down into three subcategories:

- *Recency* – pertains to the last time a payment was late. The more time that passes, the better.

- *Frequency* – this implies how often a borrower pays. One late payment looks a lot better than a dozen.

- *Severity* – a payment 30 days late is not as serious as a payment that is 60 days or 120 days late.

Debt that has been turned over to a collection agency does not represent a good record. Judgments, foreclosures, repossessions, charge-offs, bankruptcies, and collections are credit score killers. The more recent, frequent and severe the reported negative items, the bigger the impact is underscored.

How to remove such negative items will be further discussed in this book. You can also improve this aspect of your score by paying your bills on time. The more accounts you have paid as agreed, to offset the ones you don't, the more you will be able to help your score.

FICO keeps an eye on both revolving loans, and installment loans. The scores are very essential since FICO scores make the lending process for a consumer, to mortgages, student loans, and credit cards. The weight on each loan varies between individual, and FICO indicates that defaulting on a larger installment loan such as a mortgage may have a bigger impact to damage a credit score more than a severely smaller revolving loan.

If a borrower has late payments reported on their credit, it can be offset by adding new positive accounts and making sure there are many accounts that a consumer pays as agreed. This can help offset the accounts not paid as agreed. As a whole, a borrower should make consistent and timely payments. Now, consider the mortgage. How many types of mortgage accounts can you use to offset one late payment? It is a different type of account with greater responsibility, backed by collateral, namely the property.

Credit Utilization

This category denotes the percentage of available credit that has been borrowed. Though we can only boost our scores by 30 percent, it's still a vitally important element of the five listed.

Credit cards and revolving accounts are essential to actively boost the FICO score. I often tell people your past can no longer affect your score; the damage has been done. This category's real focus is on how you are actively using credit.

It is sometimes referred to as "amounts owed" or "total debts," however, they go hand in hand. For the sake of clarity, let's say these are two sub-categories in this key element. Let's start with the amount owed. Borrowers need to be mindful of the current debt carried, credit cards that are maxed-out, how many accounts with balances one has, how much the available credit is being used and more.

If it is overextended, then a consumer is more likely to miss future payments. To further explain, here is an example:

"A customer has a MasterCard with a credit limit of $10,000, and they have spent $2,000 of it. This signifies a 20 percent credit utilization ratio, which implies that the lower the ratio, the higher the credit scores."

According to FICO, people with the best scores tend to average about a 7 percent credit utilization ratio. However, 10 to 20 percent usage is acceptable. This rule of thumb applies to each individual credit card as well as the overall level of amounts owed.

We can say that the five elements of the FICO score can be enhanced or minimized based on a consumer's credit behavior. Credit usage is just an algorithm actively working on the entire FICO scoring formula. Therefore, if a consumer is looking for a quick credit score boost, they need to pay down any amounts they can. We really don't see this with on-time payments or any other category in the FICO model.

Adding credit cards to your report with high limits can also significantly and quickly raise scores, sometimes as much as 100 points or more. Nonetheless, closed accounts do not help and can hurt if there is a balance remaining, which brings us to total debts. A long-perpetuated myth has been to close accounts that are not in use. Consequently, this will hurt consumers in several ways since overall and individual account utilization plays a major role in credit-scoring. If consumers close old accounts, it actually contributes to the increase of the overall utilization rate, which can cause the score to decrease.

As seen in the five elements, payment history and credit utilization make up nearly two-thirds of the FICO score. To simplify, with FICO, the 30 percent of the credit score of a borrower is based on credit utilization, and 35 percent is based on payment history.

Anything above 30 percent of the borrower's limit being used will eventually lower their credit scores. This means that if a consumer is over-utilizing their revolving accounts, they can damage scores as much as if they were actually late with their payments each month. Hence, if a consumer pays their bill on time and does not carry big balances, the two-thirds of the total score can pave the way towards a better credit score.

Most credit card companies have now started to add what-if simulators for free. I highly recommend you go through a few simulations to get an idea of how your scores can be affected by either paying down your credit cards or maxing them out.

Age of Credit History

The third category is based on the length of time each account of the borrower has been open and the account's most recent action. Therefore, it answers how long you've had credit. Consumers need to be cautious about how long they have had established credit, from their oldest to newest account, on average of all their accounts.

This is why it is sometimes called, "length of credit history" or simply, "depth of credit." This may be less important than the previous factors, but it still matters for the following reasons:

- This is the 3rd largest aspect of the score calculation (15%).

- The average age of accounts is another important reason to keep all accounts open since it considers the age of the oldest accounts and the average age of all accounts.

- It is possible to have a good credit score with a short history, even if, typically, the longer, the better.

A longer credit history can provide more information and can also offer a better image of a long-term financial behavior. As a result, consumers without a history should begin using credit, and those who have credit should make sure they are able to maintain long-standing accounts.

If a person is new to credit, then there is little they can do to improve this component in relation to their credit score. No newly added accounts can be back-dated to improve this score's aspect. Thus, it is impossible for a consumer who is new to credit to have a perfect credit score.

Young people, students, and others can still have high credit scores as long as the other factors are positive. Some can get added as an authorized user to a family member's account that has been in long-standing status that can, sooner or later, help improve the aspect of the score. Keep in mind when we talk about FICO scores we are essentially dealing with risk. With little to no history, the unknown becomes risky by default.

Furthermore, credit reporting agencies will calculate an account as inactive if there has not been any activity in the most recent 6-month period of time. An inactive account does not benefit a borrower's credit score as much as an active account.

It is essential to make sure that consumers use each of their accounts at least once every 6 months. It is also important to be aware that credit issuers must reserve the money offered in credit limits for their client's use. As a consequence, they do not like having accounts sitting dormant because they are not generating money. If an account sits dormant for a long enough time, many creditors nowadays will cancel the account due to inactivity.

New Credit

The fourth category is also known as inquiries or new credit history. New credit is not always a bad thing. It shows how a borrower actively applied for credit in the past year.

The scoring models look for "rate shopping." Shopping for a mortgage or an auto loan may cause multiple lenders to request a borrower's credit report many times, even though a person is only looking for one loan. Additionally, opening new accounts is not recommended if a consumer applies for many credit lines at the same time or within a short period of time. Consumers need to be careful about this, particularly if it cannot be backed up by a long credit history. The score in this component factors in the following:

- How many accounts has the consumer applied for recently?

- How many new accounts the consumer has opened?

- How much time has passed since the consumer opened an account?

- And most importantly, whether the consumer was approved or denied credit.

According to myFico.com, people with six inquiries or more on their credit reports are eight times more likely to declare bankruptcy compared to people with no inquiries on their reports. FICO suggests that borrowers should only take an inquiry or additional credit when it is needed, if they must have it or when it financially makes sense.

Even though for most people, a credit inquiry really won't have an impact on their credit score, groupings of inquiries will adversely affect scores. Large numbers of inquiries also mean greater risk. Promotional insurance, employment, and queries do not count against the consumer. However, inquiries can have a greater impact if the borrower has a few accounts or short credit history.

Auto dealers are notorious for running 3 to 15 credit reports. This is referred to as, "shotgunning" the credit. Luckily, to compensate for this, the score counts multiple auto and mortgage specific inquiries in any 30-45-day period as just one inquiry.

The specific calculation for cut-off dates and types is confusing to most consumers. This will be explained more in detail with the succeeding chapters. Hence, a consumer is advised to be cautious in this aspect since careless behavior could suggest they are in financial trouble and need significant access to lots of credit.

I want to help clear up a few misconceptions about inquiries on a credit report. First of all, if you have anything less than a 640 FICO score, you should not apply for new credit. So, when are inquiries a big deal? There are two types of inquiries: hard pulls for credit loans, and soft pulls for non-credit-related reporting.

Here is the thing, most people worry about inquiries for the wrong reason, mainly for the loss of points. Overall inquiries account for 10 percent of your score. The max you could lose is 55 points if you actually maxed out this category.

Here is where inquiries are a BIG deal, even with A1 credit: applying for multiple accounts within a short period of time will eventually get denied based on that alone, even with perfect credit.

A rule of thumb I use is not to apply for more than four accounts within a six month period. After two years, the inquiries fall off, and after one year, they don't have an impact on your score. If you get denied the first time for any reason, DO NOT apply for any new credit.

If you have bad credit, why keep applying, as if credit and Vegas have something in common? This is not a slot machine. You can't continue to pull the lever and expect an approval. Inquiries can do less damage to your score, but more damage to your ability to actually get credit period. So, ask yourself, who cares about scores when you jeopardize getting denied credit altogether? Inquiries are a big deal, but not the way most people see them.

Credit Mix

The last category is somewhat vague on what it means; however, according to FICO, past data representing a range of debt specifies that the consumer can handle all sorts of credit. A borrower with a good mix of revolving credit and installment loans generally characterizes less risk for lenders.

It is recommended that a consumer should have a balance of both revolving debts such as credit cards, installment loans such as auto loans, mortgages and others. Scoring models want to see a healthy mix of credit, which is sometimes referred to as "types of credit used." To further illustrate, here is an example:

Credit bureaus will give a higher score if the borrower has an open mortgage, three credit cards, one auto loan and a small amount of other open accounts. However, if the borrower has tons of credit cards, several mortgages and four auto loans, the scores will be lowered.

The point is, too much credit is risky and too little credit is even riskier.

As shown in the example, the preferred number of credit cards reporting is three. A consumer should not have more than two mortgages or auto loans reporting. Installment loans also score better if a borrower has two or less.

FICO considers a borrower's credit cards, finance company accounts, installment loans, and mortgage loans, but it is not required to have one of each type. It is also not a good idea to open different credit accounts a consumer does not really intend to use.

The credit mix may not present a big factor in defining a borrower's FICO score; nevertheless, it will be more significant if the credit report does not have a lot of information upon which to base a score.

FICO scores will consider the different types of credit used, as it indicates how a borrower manages them responsibly. The flexibility of a borrower to handle a diversified set of credit accounts can be seen through this category.

The types of credit used may sometimes be ignored by borrowers, but even if it has the same percentage as new credit, it contributes to the overall FICO score. It is essential that consumers understand their FICO scores and how it is calculated because it can help them know whether or not they can qualify for low rates on their next loan.

Also, keep in mind that each consumer has specific score-cards they are being filed under. I will explore this subject a little more in later chapters.

Chapter 4

TRENDED DATA

"Never spend your money before you have earned it."

--Thomas Jefferson

Recent years of economic instability have affected the fast evolution of consumers. This makes it crucial for lenders to understand their borrowers from the deepest and most current perspective available because the standards are tightened within the mortgage industry. Consequently, mortgage professionals agreed that more detailed data and insights from consumers were needed to create better control and make the industry go back to a safer lending environment.

In the U.S market, Fannie Mae and Freddie Mac set most of the guidelines for lending standards, as the majority of mortgage loans are processed through the underwriting machines of these two government-owned agencies.

Trended data is a detailed record of a consumer's credit history. The credit bureaus are using their trended data to create new products they can sell to lenders that better analyze consumer risk. Experian sells a trended data product called Trended Solutions, Equifax offers Dimension, and TransUnion has CreditVision. It includes the historical payment amount for each month going back 30 months under TransUnion's CreditVision or 24 months under Equifax Dimensions. It also considers the amount owed, minimum payment and payments made. The expanded information on the consumer allows a smarter and thorough analysis of the borrower's credit history.

The data helps creditworthy borrowers find access to mortgage credit and sustainable homeownership. As a result, it is the best tool industrialized by the credit reporting agencies since the beginning of the credit score. The trended data enables lenders to differentiate between transactors and revolvers. Transactors are borrowers who pay their credit card balances in full every month. On the other hand, the revolvers carry credit card balances from month to month.

Who will benefit and who will lose from the inclusion of trended data?

Consumers who pay their balance in full every month and do not use their credit card to borrow money will certainly benefit from this. The best representation for trended data has been credit utilization. Utilization is the measurement of a borrower's total credit balance versus the credit limit.

If utilization is high, it is more likely that the borrower is assumed to be in credit card debt. On the contrary, using credit utilization is somehow an unsharpened tool since there are circumstances where consumers max out their credit cards every month but pay the balance in full. Such events can be affected by the current scoring technique. Financial and lending institutions will benefit since the data provides lenders a better way to predict risk and create a lending policy. Those who pay their statement balance in full and on time will have good scores.

Furthermore, borrowers who are not able to afford to pay in full will face negative consequences. A credit card debt that cannot be paid will have a damaging influence over the score. The way to keep good scores is by keeping credit utilization low and paying bills on time every month. However, it is dependent upon the lender and how they use the trended data. Credit utilization techniques may become useful in some ways. A borrower who is in credit card debt, or has a historical record of staying in debt, may expect a severely damaged score.

Consequently, the use of trended data will be rewarding for consumers who religiously pay their credit balances in full monthly. People who maintain good financial health will greatly benefit as well and can lead to an excellent score. It is advised that borrowers should be mindful if they are in credit card debt.

Since the trended data shows credit usage over time, lenders would prefer borrowers who keep a zero balance or pay more than the minimum payment every month. It is also used for risk assessment, as it is a further piece of information used by lenders for underwriting mortgage loans.

When deciding whether to approve a loan and how much to charge in fees, Fannie Mae's underwriting software considers several factors. These factors include credit scores; overall credit report, which includes the payment history; credit utilization and outstanding balances; the size of the down payment, for purchase or refinanced loan; type of dwelling; loan-to-value ratios and debt-to-income ratios.

It is important consumers understand that trended data does not change the credit scores that are used by the mortgage industry. It is simply an added quantity of information that lenders use.

The industry's leading automated underwriting system is called Desktop Underwriter (DU). It has provided lenders a complete risk assessment that defines whether a loan meets the eligibility requirements of the government agencies. It results in a fair and objective evaluation which applies the same criteria to every mortgage loan application it considers.

Chapter 5

THE MORTGAGE OVERVIEW

I never attempt to make money on the stock market. I buy on the assumption that they could close the market the next day and not reopen it for ten years.

--Warren Buffett

UnderwritingGuidelines for the Average Mortgage Loan

1.Income

Income is one of the most important variables a lender will examine because it is used to repay the loan. Income is reviewed for the type of work, length of employment, educational training required and an opportunity for advancement. An underwriter will look at the source of income and the likelihood of its continuance to arrive at a gross monthly figure. The following are different sources of income and types of income:

- *Salary and Hourly Wages* are calculated on a gross monthly basis, prior to income tax deductions.

- *Part-time and Second Job Income* is not usually considered unless it is in place for 12 to 24 straight months. Lenders view part-time income as a strong compensating factor.

- *Commission, Bonus, and Overtime Income* can only be used if received for two previous years. Furthermore, an employer must verify that it is likely to continue. A 24-month average figure is used.

- *Retirement and Social Security Income* must continue for at least three years into the future to be considered. If it is tax-free, it can be grossed up to an equivalent gross monthly figure by multiplying the net amount by 1.20 percent.

- *Alimony and Child Support Income* must be received for the previous 12 months and continue for the next 36 months. Lenders will require a divorce decree and a court printout to verify on-time payments.

- *Notes Receivable, Interest, Dividend and Trust Income* will be the proof of receiving funds for

12 previous months is required. Documentation showing income due for 3 more years is also necessary.

- *Rental Income* cannot come from a primary residence roommate. The only acceptable source is from an investment property. A lender will use 75 percent of the monthly rent and subtract ownership expenses. The Schedule E of a tax return is used to verify the figures. If a home has been rented recently, a copy of a current month-to-month lease is acceptable.

- *Automobile Allowance and Expense Account Reimbursements* are verified with 2 years of tax returns and reduced by actual expenses listed on the income tax return Schedule C.

- *Education Expense Reimbursements* are not considered income. It is only viewed as a slight compensating factor.

- *Self-employment Income* is also considered. However, lenders are very careful in reviewing self-employed borrowers. Two years minimum ownership is necessary because it is considered a representative sample. Lenders use a two-year average monthly income figure from the adjusted gross income on the tax returns. A lender may also add back additional income for depreciation and one-time capital expenses.

Self-employed borrowers often have difficulty qualifying for a mortgage due to large expense write-offs. A good solution to this challenge used to be the No Income Verification Loan, but there are very few of these available anymore given the tightened lending standards in the current economy. NIV loan programs can be studied in the Mortgage Program section of the library.

2. Debt and Liabilities

Lenders need to make sure there is enough income for the proposed mortgage payment after other revolving and installment debts are paid. Therefore, an applicant's liabilities are reviewed for cash flow. It must then be remembered that:

- All loans, leases, and credit cards are factored into the debt calculation. Utilities, insurance, food, clothing, schooling, and others are not.

- If a loan has less than 10 months remaining, a lender will usually disregard it.

- The minimum monthly payment listed on a credit card bill is the figure used, not the payment made.

- An applicant who co-borrowed for a friend or relative is accountable for the payment. If the applicant can show 12 months of on-time canceled checks from the co-borrower, the debt will not count.

- Loans can be paid off to qualify for a mortgage, but credit cards sometimes cannot, which varies depending on the lender. The reason for this is that if the credit card is paid off, the credit line still exists, and the borrower can run up debt after the loan is closed.

- A borrower with fewer liabilities is thought to demonstrate superior cash management skills.

3. Credit History

Most lenders require a residential mortgage credit report (RMCR) from the three main credit bureaus, namely TransUnion, Equifax, and Experian. These credit reporting agencies will order one report which is a blending of all three credit bureaus. It is easier to read compared to the individual reports. This "blended credit report" also searches public records for liens, judgments, bankruptcies, and foreclosures.

Given the credit report in hand, an underwriter studies the applicant's credit to determine the likelihood of receiving an on-time mortgage payment. Several studies have shown that past performance is a reflection of future expectations. Hence, most lenders now prefer to use a national credit scoring system, typically the FICO score, to evaluate credit risk. The mortgage lending process, despite being lenient before, has considerably tightened the lending standards.

A person with excellent credit, good stability, and sufficient, documentable income to make the payments comfortably will usually qualify for an A-paper loan.

A-paper loans, sometimes referred to as conforming loans, make up the majority of loans in the U.S. These are loans that must follow the guidelines set by Fannie Mae or Freddie Mac in order to be sold by the lender. Such loans must meet established and strict requirements regarding maximum loan amount, down payment amount, borrower income, credit requirements, and suitable properties.

Loans that do not meet the credit and/or income requirements of A-paper loans are known as non-conforming loans'. These are often referred to as B-, C- and D-paper loans depending on the borrower's credit history and financial capacity.

Provided Below Are Some Rules of Thumb
Most Lenders Follow

- 12 plus months of positive credit will usually get you into an A-paper loan program, depending on the overall credit. FHA loans usually follow this guideline more often than conventional loans.

- Unpaid collections, judgments, and charge-offs must be paid prior to closing an A-paper loan. The only exception is if the debt was due to the death of a primary wage earner, or the bill was a medical expense.

- If a borrower has negotiated an acceptable payment plan and has made on-time payments for 6 to 12 months, a lender may not require a debt to be paid off prior to closing.

- Credit items are usually reported for 7 years. Bankruptcies expire after 10 years.

- Foreclosures are 5 years from the completion date. From the fifth to the seventh year following the foreclosure completion date, the purchase of a principal residence is permitted with a minimum 10 percent down and 680 FICO score. The purchase of a second or investment property is not permitted for seven years. Limited cash-out refinances are permitted for all occupancy types.

- Short Sale should be two years from the completion date, and there are no exceptions or extenuating circumstances.

- Deed-in-Lieu of Foreclosure will be a four-year period from the date the deed-in-lieu is executed. From the fifth to the seventh year following the execution date.

- The borrower may purchase a property secured by a principal residence, second home or investment property with the greater of 10 percent minimum down payment or the minimum down payment required for the transaction.

Limited cash-out and cash-out refinance transactions secured by a principal residence, second home or investment property are permitted pursuant to the eligibility requirements in effect at that time.

- Chapter 7 Bankruptcy states that a borrower is eligible for an A-paper loan program four years after discharge or dismissal, provided they have re-established credit and have maintained perfect credit after the bankruptcy.

- Chapter 13 Bankruptcy states that two years from the discharge date or four years from the dismissal date borrowers will be eligible of most conforming loans.

- Multiple Bankruptcies means five years from the most recent dismissal or discharge date for borrowers with more than one filing in the past seven years.

- The good credit of a co-borrower does not offset the bad credit of a borrower.

- Credit scores usually range from 400 to 800. Changes to lending standards are occurring on a daily basis as a result of tightened lending standards and can vary from lender to lender. As a result, this information should be considered simply as a guideline.

For conforming loans, most lenders will lend down to a FICO of 620, with additional rate hits for the lower-end credit scores and loan-to-values.

- When an applicant is borrowing more than 80 percent, the possibility of going through a lending process is low if a FICO is below 680. The FHA/VA program just changed their

49

minimum required FICO to 620, unless a follower is being qualified with non-traditional credit.

- The few non-conforming loan programs that are still available typically require a 30 percent down payment with a minimum FICO of 700 for self-employed, and 650 for W-2 employees and the loan-to-value will change with the loan amount.

- A credit score below 600 may require an Alternative Credit mortgage program.

Savings and Checking Accounts

Lenders evaluate checking and savings accounts for three reasons. These reasons are as follows:

1. The more money a borrower has after closing, the greater the probability of on-time payments.

2. Most loan programs require a minimum borrower contribution.

3. Lenders want to know that consumers have invested their own funds into the house, making it less likely that they will walk away from their life's savings. They

WHO GIVES A FICO

analyze savings documents to ensure the applicant did not borrow the funds or receive a gift.

Lenders look at the following types of accounts and assets for down payment funds:

- Checking and Savings Funds requires 60 days seasoning in a bank account.

- Gifts and Grants are permitted after a borrower's minimum contribution.

- Sale of Assets means a personal property can be sold for the required contribution. The property should be appraised, and a bill of sale is required. In addition, a copy of the received check and a deposit slip are needed.

- Secured Loans are loans that are secured by property and are also an acceptable source of closing funds.

- IRA, 401K, Keogh & SEP pertains to any amount that can be accessed and is an acceptable source of funds.

- Sweat equity and cash-on-hand are generally not acceptable. FHA programs allow it in special circumstances.

51

- Sale of the previous home must close prior to a new home for the funds to be used. A lender will ask for a listing contract, sales contract, or HUD 1 closing statement.

- Debt vs. income ratio refers to the percentage of one's debt to income. It is one of the most important factors when underwriting a loan. Lenders have determined that a house payment should not exceed approximately 30 percent of gross monthly income.

Gross monthly income is income before taxes are taken out. Furthermore, a house payment plus minimum monthly revolving and installment debt should be less than 40 percent of gross monthly income.

To illustrate further here is an example

If an applicant has $4,500 gross monthly income, the maximum mortgage payment is: $4,500 x .30 = $1,350

The Total Debts come to:

Car	$500
Visa	$20
Sears	$30
MasterCard	$75

$625 per month	

52

Remember, the total debts (mortgage plus other debts) must be less than or equal to 40 percent of their gross monthly income, which leads to $4,500 x .40 = $1,800

The maximum amount of debt the borrower can have it $1,800; which is debts and mortgage payments combined. The question is whether the borrower can keep all their debts and have the maximum mortgage payment allowed. The answer is *NO*.

In this case, since the borrower has high debts, they must adjust the maximum mortgage payment downward, because:

Debts   = $625

Mortgage   = $1350

$1,975 which is more than the $1,800 (40% of gross income) as calculated above.

The maximum mortgage payment is therefore:

$1,800 - $625 (monthly debt) = $1,175

Mortgage insurance has become a direct factor in qualifying for a home as well. This insurance compensates the lender for losses if the borrower defaults on the loan due to the risk of consumers who put less than 20 percent down on a home. Programs such as FHA and Conventional loans allow borrowers to put as low as 3 percent down on conventional loans and 3.5 percent down on FHA loans. However, they must retain some form of mortgage insurance.

Since Mortgage insurance involves risk, credit is also a direct correlation to the payment you will be issued contingent upon your credit score. Ouch! This can cause some consumers who buy the same home with the same exact down payment in the same neighborhood to have an entirely different payment altogether. Most consumers do not consider the mortgage insurance as a factor in the monthly payment, but this can be the deal breaker when you consider overall debt to income ratios in these loan programs.

The problem with FHA loans is that the mortgage insurance will remain during the life of the loan. However, conventional loans will allow you to cancel the mortgage insurance payment if the home reaches 80 percent loan-to-value. Keep in mind, you will still have to order an appraisal to verify the home has reached the 80 percent mark. On a conventional loan, the two most common types of private mortgage insurance areborrower-paid, and lender-paid private mortgage insurance.

Borrower-paid mortgage insurance allows the borrower to pay a percentage rate of the principal balance ranging anywhere from .32 percent to 1.20 percent.

Lender-paid mortgage insurance is paid by the lender and is often calculated into the interest rate and not as a separate payment.

I strongly recommend that you go over your options with a competent mortgage loan originator to find out what scenario fits your needs.

Chapter **6**

THE VANTAGE SCORE

Opportunity is missed by most people because it is dressed in overalls and looks like work.

--Thomas Edison

Threads the credit bureaus have designed and released their own credit scoring model called VantageScore. It is a consumer score used by Credit Karma. The scores emerged in the market March of 2006. All of the three main credit reporting agencies use the same formula to calculate it.

There is also an increasing number of lenders that are beginning to adopt this scoring model. In March of 2013, Vantage Score 3.0 was introduced, and it is the most recent version of the scoring model.

Vantage Score claims that their latest version provides scores to general consumers and helps millions of borrowers who may not have a credit profile with alternative models. As a result, it is used by many lenders and financial institutions.

Vantage scores, like other credit scores, consists of calculations. It relies entirely on the credit bureau's information about the consumer. The scores are also influenced by the credit behavior of borrowers. Since it predicts the likelihood of a consumer to pay, it will also consider how payments are paid on time, debt balances, credit history and other inquiries on credit reports.

Additionally, it has variables that are similar to a FICO score, yet it also has its own differentiation. To further illustrate, the variables of a Vantage score are presented below:

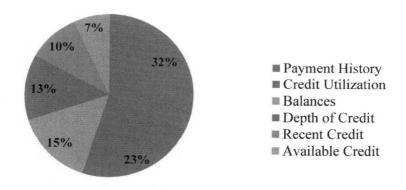

VANTAGE SCORES VS. FICO SCORE

The difference between FICO scores and Vantage scores are long and technical. An awareness of what the difference is between the two scores and how it can affect credit is important. The differences in score range, scoring criteria, scorecards, and authorized accounts will be discussed.

Score Range

The score range of FICO and Vantage are different. It is mentioned in the previous chapters that FICO scores range from 300-850 and tends to vary depending on the credit information from each bureau. FICO Scores also have the tendency for a momentous effect on each of the credit spectrum.

When using FICO scores, once the consumers start building credit and improving their scores, it will be easier to further increase their scores. The higher the scores are, the lesser the impact of minor negative marks will be.

On the other hand, Vantage scores range from 501-990. The credit bureaus have taken a number of steps to make the scores seem attractive to lenders. Most of the details are technical and in language that is quite difficult to explain. The credit bureaus have taken special steps that will reduce the score variations that normally occur between bureaus.

Therefore, Vantage scores were built using a profile of data across the three bureaus and through what they refer to as "characteristic leveling." The bureaus have essentially recognized the broad sampling of data from various sources, which they used to create an algorithm to interpret the varying data consistently.

The credit bureaus were strategic since they used the data they owned to their advantage. They also designed a way to analyze their data in a way that only they are capable of.

Scoring Criteria

The previous chapters discussed thoroughly the scoring criteria of FICO. There will be fewer variations in scores between bureaus when they use the Vantage score. To better compare, the illustration below shows the differences between the two scores:

Vantage Score		FICO Score	
Payment History	32%	Payment History	35%
Credit Utilization	23%	Credit Utilization	30%
Balances	15%	Age of Credit History	15%
Depth of Credit	13%	New Credit	10%
Recent Credit	10%	Credit Mix	10%
Available Credit	7%		
Total	100%	Total	100%

As shown in the illustration, when comparing Vantage scores to FICO Scores, the score may be a little less top-heavy. This calculation is based on statistics showing the number of consumer's in each credit score range on VantageScore.com. There is a 3 percent difference on payment history and 7 percent difference for credit utilization.

FICO scores specify recent credit searches of only 10 percent, while with Vantage Scores, 30 percent is allotted to depth of credit, recent credit, and available credit. This makes Vantage scores appear to be more complicated when compared to FICO Scores.

Several newly-opened accounts can hurt a FICO score before they can eventually help. Vantage scores are different since they have 23 percent for credit utilization, 7 percent for available credit and 15 percent for balances, which will give a total of 45 percent. This can greatly affect borrowers who are over-utilizing their credit.

With FICO scores, credit utilization, along with credit limits, are analyzed to determine credit usage, which is the result of giving only 30% for those criteria. The lower percentage for the Vantage score under credit utilization means a positive effect of methods dealing with debt to credit ratio could slightly diminish.

Score Cards

It was mentioned beforehand that the FICO scoring model uses a "scorecard." The scorecards are used to score consumers in relation to the performances of others in the same category. An example scenario would be if borrowers have a bankruptcy on their credit reports, they would be scored with regards to how they perform compared to their peers or others who also have a bankruptcy on their credit.

If a consumer, on the other hand, likes to take good care of their credit and opens a new positive account after a bankruptcy, it could cause their credit to go up significantly through the scorecard effect. The increase is due to the fact that the consumers will be doing substantially better than others in the same category.

The Vantage scores use scorecards as well and will likely have a similar effect on the scoring behavior. Bankruptcy scorecards are also available in Vantage scores and will probably have the same effects. Even if the scorecards are different between the two scoring systems, they are expected to have similar effects since the scorecard system was originally designed to create that exact effect. It looks at people in a certain category and determines how the best behave, how the worst behaves and tries to figure which group a consumer can fit into.

Authorized Accounts

FICO takes authorized user accounts into consideration as long as they are legitimate. Furthermore, they try to rule out purchased authorized accounts that were popular before known as "seasoned trade lines." Authorized user accounts work very well amongst married couples.

However, Vantage scores do not and will not take authorized user accounts into consideration. This means that if you are not the primary user on an account, then the account will not be considered in calculating your credit score.

Chapter *7*

BUILDING A SOLID SCORE

"If we command our wealth, we shall be rich and free.
If our wealth commands us, we are poor indeed."

--Edmund Burke

FICO scores typically range from 300 to 850, meaning we only have 550 points to work with. Negative items will only affect 45 percent of your overall score; that's 247 points. In order to have a ballpark figure of where to start, here is a list of the eight types of negative items that will affect your scores from the greatest to the least:

1. Bankruptcies can have the most drastic effect on the credit score due to the nature of the bankruptcy. Keep in mind, when a consumer files for bankruptcy, they are putting accounts that were once on the credit report in good standing. All of those accounts will now be included in the bankruptcy.

Any positive information those accounts previously retained will no longer be counted as positive. If the Bankruptcy is done with a proper strategy, you can actually cause scores to go up. If those accounts were reporting negatively and if you still have positive credit to lean on once those accounts are completely closed.

Bankruptcies can impact your credit scores by anywhere from 100 to 240 points, depending on where your credit score is calculated.

2. Foreclosure is the legal process of a mortgage company taking possession of a mortgaged property when a homeowner fails to make payments. The range a foreclosure can affect FICO scores is 80 to 160 points.

3. Repossessions are just as serious as foreclosures because they both represent a borrower defaulting on installment loans. This means your scores are being affected by late payments for a period of time, then being impacted by the adverse claim of a creditor taking legal action on the same account.

4. Judgments can be very cumbersome to deal with because these are accounts that go to public records, as well as bankruptcies and foreclosures. These accounts can damage your credit up to 150 points.

5. Collections accounts are the most common account type seen on the credit report. The most common collection

is medical collections. You can lose up to 90 points on a collection account depending on your current FICO score.

6. Charge-offs are accounts that creditors place on the report with any attempt to collect the debt. They write them off as an unresolved debt for the tax benefit. It's often best to settle these accounts before they go to that stage.

7. Late Payments can be just as devastating to a credit score, depending on how late the payments are. If a consumer is 30 days late, it will take nine months to recover from the late payment. If a consumer is 60 to 180 days late, it will affect him differently as well. Late payments can reduce a credit score up to 80 points

8. Inquiries may have their own category, but these are very minimal compared to the other negative items previously listed. Out of 550 points in the FICO scoring model, inquiries make up 10 percent. So, if you had a perfect credit score, the most you would lose for multiple inquiries would be 55 points. In one hard credit pull, maybe seven points at most. So, don't lose sleep over inquiries. Lose sleep over denied credit.

So, the question is, how are we going to increase our FICO score when there is so much to lose? Where can we begin if there are so many moving parts to this five-category equation? First, we must start with the basics. If you don't have any positive credit reporting, I can assume your scores are very low. This means you must start with a secure credit card that does not require a hard pull on the application. You will need at least 3 to have a full FICO scorecard.

Next, make on-time payments for 6 straight months. This means you are going to actively use your credit every month. Make sure you keep your utilization as low as possible.

Sure, there are some good practices in raising credit scores, but what if you have so many negative items listed on your credit report? Always remember, the efforts you make to raise your scores won't matter that much because the black marks on your credit reports signal a heavier burden for the FICO scoring system. When there are too many black marks listed, you will have lower credit scores even if you are practicing good credit habits.

All Americans are entitled to a free credit report from each of the major credit bureaus once a year. Only a handful of people realize the importance of acquiring such reports, but driven people, like you, who are serious about finding out why their credit score is such a mess, know the importance of reviewing theirs.

There's only one person to blame if the negative items on your credit report are not removed, and that is you. Once you have the credit reports, review each entry carefully and look for any errors in your accounts. Here are some guide questions when you check your credit report:

- Do all of the accounts listed belong to you?

- Are there any delayed payments listed, even if you paid your balances in a timely manner?

- Do any of your previous loans and mortgages appear unpaid and long overdue, even if you have settled them in full?

- Are there any reports of bankruptcies and court charges that have exceeded the 10-year allowable imit?

- Are there any reports about collection debts that have been paid, but exceeded the 7-year reporting limit?

If you can see any entries that fit into these questions, you must by all means necessary have them removed or altered by the concerned lenders, authorities, and credit card issuers.

If possible, keep all your payment receipts all year round to see whether the credit providers are reporting correct items on your credit report.

If you do not check your credit report at least once a year, all of these abusive and neglecting lenders will continue to post black marks on your credit report that shouldn't be there in the first place.

If your credit score falls below the qualifying mark of 720 and above because of these erroneous entries, you won't be able to secure the best credit terms available.

When your mediocre credit scores are taken into consideration by the lenders, you will be getting higher interest rates for installment plans, credit cards, housing loans, auto loans, mortgages and health insurances. If this happens, you will be spending thousands of dollars trying to pay for the interests alone.

However, if you continue checking your credit report religiously, you could save thousands from paying these interest rates. Think about it! Wouldn't it be great to get pre-approved for the best credit terms available? Go ahead and start repairing your credit report so that you can get started with lighter payment plans for the items you desire the most.

Establishing Good Credit Scores

Good Credit scores are essential to our way of life whether you actively participate in improving your score or not. While the common story is always about those who have fallen into debt or financial trouble and as a result have seen a somersault in their credit scores, there is this other class of people who do not have any credit history.

So, the question is, how are we going to increase our FICO score when there is so much to lose? Where can we begin if the FICO score has so many moving parts to the five-category equation? First, we must start with the basics. If you don't have any positive credit reporting, I can assume your scores are very low. This means you must start with secure credit card accounts that do not require a hard pull on the application. You will need at least three revolving accounts to have a full FICO scores card.

It sounds impossible but it is true that in these ages, there are a lot of people like this with little or no credit history. This is true in the case of housewives, young people, students and dependents whose financial needs have been taken care of by others or who have not found it necessary at anytime to seek credit for any purpose at all.

Now, your thoughts at this point may be: why should a person in such financial "nirvana" need to bother with getting a credit score or history? After all, isn't it nothing but trouble? Something you acquire and spend the rest of your life babysitting?

Though these questions might be valid, there are logical reasons for some people to seek a credit history. For instance, take the case of a new divorcee or a young person. It is widely known that in order to benefit from some job opportunities, some kinds of accommodation and a few other things, a healthy credit history is required.

If you fall into this category, then this is for you, building good credit scores and a credit history is actually as simple as A-B-C.

Make sure you keep your utilization as low as possible. This is simple enough, but most people can't follow these straightforward instructions without either over-using the credit or missing a payment.

Use the card for buying gas and other small expenses, and make sure you conscientiously pay the card down to 1 percent at most. We don't want to pay it off completely, because we want to show that the card is active every month

Note that when applying for a secure card, apply for the ones that report to all three credit bureaus. It is important that the secure card company doesn't pull your credit. There are several that won't do a credit check because the security deposit is all that is required.

When you are rebuilding your credit it is best to start with one card. If you pay this regularly, you would surely get offers for more (which you must treat the same way as the first).

The financial institutions and others would rate you higher if, on your credit report, they see that you can handle different kinds of loans well, so it is also advisable to take out a small loan and also pay it regularly. This will be an installment loan to help the mix of credit category. It is not really necessary that you use it so you can keep the money in a separate account and pay off from there.

If you regularly and faithfully keep up to this schedule, over a 24-month period, you would see the results on your credit report. This procedure is also applicable to those who have bad credit ratings and are looking for a way to steadily build up. Avoid closing any credit accounts; there are other methods you can use if you simply don't want to use the card any longer. Remember, our goal is to build a credit history that displays a predictable pattern of responsible credit usage.

Maintain Your Good Credit

Once you've been approved for a home loan or credit card, the most important thing is to keep control of it. You want to achieve your financial goals without getting too far into debt. Keep track of your spending: Keep track of the checks you've written, debit and credit card transactions, and ATM card usage. Review your monthly statements when they arrive, and report any possible discrepancies immediately.

Don't exceed your credit limit on lines of credit and credit cards. Your available credit is how much credit you have left on a line of credit or credit card; it is your credit limit minus your outstanding balance. Be careful to keep your spending below this amount. Following the "20/10 rule," it is a good practice not to let your credit card debt exceed more than 20 percent of your total yearly income after taxes. Each month, don't have more than 10 percent of your monthly take-home pay in credit card payments.

Have an emergency fund. Keep at least a 15 percent cushion of available credit in case of emergency. Or better yet, keep an emergency savings fund of three to six months' living expenses in a liquid, interest-earning account. That way, if you lose your job or have a big unexpected expense, you don't have to borrow more than you're comfortable repaying.

Pay what you owe. Always pay at least your minimum monthly payment on-time every month. By paying more than the minimum - or better yet, the full balance each month -

you will reduce your finance charges. Be sure not to skip any payments.

• Make timely payments

Timely payment is one of the best ways to establish yourself as a good credit risk to future lenders.

Be organized. Put all your bills in one place so you don't lose them or forget about them. Keep a list of the bills you have due, and if it will make it easier for you to remember to pay them, make them due on the same day each month. (Contact your lender to see if you can change your payment due date.)

Pay attention to the payment due dates. Mail your payment, or schedule an online payment through your bank's bill pay service at least one week before the due date. Sign up for automatic payments. Using automatic loan payments from your checking account is a simple, convenient way to regularly make your payments. Be sure to schedule them according to your pay schedule to ensure you have sufficient funds for the payment when it is drafted.

Keep your contact information current. If you're moving, remember to fill out the change of address form on your statement or update it online to ensure that your statement goes to your new address.

- ## **Stay In Touch With Your Creditors**

Contact your lenders immediately if you fall behind on your payments. Most creditors are willing to set up alternative payment options, especially if you inform them right away of your situation.

Chapter **8**

HOW IMPORTANT IS THE FICO SCORE?

"If you would be wealthy, think of saving as well as getting."

--Ben Franklin

In this chapter, I will go into more detail about the different types of scoring models used by FICO in specific industries. Though there are different scoring models outside of the FICO score, 90 percent of lenders will use the FICO score as an evaluation of creditworthiness. When most people think about the FICO score, they think about one score or one calculation being used. There are six varieties in the FICO system lenders commonly use:

1. The Generic FICO Score

2. The FICO Mortgage Industry Option Score

3. The Auto Industry Option Score

4. The FICO Bankcard Score

5. The FICO Installment Loan Score

6. The FICO Personal Finance Score

The basic FICO formula is still intact even with these different varieties, but the emphasis is they are industry-specific. To keep it simple, there is the base version, such as the FICO 08, and the industry-specific versions like the Mortgage Industry Option Score. The best place to check the specific version to your lending needs visit MYFICO.com.

My intent is not to complicate the process or confuse you; I'm simply shedding light on the possibility that lenders are using a score far different from the ones you receive from most consumer credit reporting websites.

There is even a score specific to the insurance industry called the credit-based insurance score. This score is used to predict the likelihood of a consumer not paying premiums on-time and the actual premium payments itself. Insurance companies also utilize this score to determine if an applicant will be accepted or denied for insurability. Imagine that when you consider all the various types of insurance we actually use. At the end of the day, it's all about a calculation of risk.

In order to understand the financial downturn, credit reports and legal debt dumping, some historical backgroundon how these companies all work illegally should be considered. Search for terms such as: "the gig is up," and "money the Federal Reserve and you" to get the real deal on how money works and how you've been cheated for your whole life!

You're getting there now! You know we have fake money so collectors can never take money from you because none was loaned. Search the term "FTC debt video" to see how easy it is to record those collection calls and get free money when collectors start talking funny. Another search term like "man wins $1.5 million from collector" shows how you can even do it accidentally!

In case you didn't get rich by recording the phone calls, you can still dump the debt by answering those collection notices with the demand for a proof of debt letter. Doesn't get much simpler than that does it? The plastic is gone, so let's do the 850 FICO score stuff.

By now, you've probably figured out every thing is totally opposite from what you thought. The same thing is true of the credit reporting industry. According to section 609 of the Fair Credit Reporting Act, they must have verifiable proof that what they're reporting is true. You don't beg them to correct some inaccuracy. You tell them to show you verifiable proof or take it off your report.

Time to celebrate your new knowledge base so throw a little Orville Redenbacher's Pop Secret in the nuke and think about this: you don't need a credit report to dump the cards.

Make a fortune off the collector while you're dumping the debt, get a free credit report, then jump on the reporting agencies and tell them to take anything you want off your credit history.

How often do you check your report?

Checking your credit report is vital when it comes to preparing your financial future. Online resources make it easier than ever for you to review your report, and checking it is free. But how do you know when and how often you need to review your report? If you are preparing for a financed or major purchase, you will want to review your report prior to applying for a loan or line of credit.

The interest rate you pay on a mortgage loan, auto loan and your credit card interest rates all are determined by your credit score. Keep in mind that three out of four credit reports contain errors. Those mistakes could be negatively affecting your credit score without your knowledge. Review your report closely and keep an eye out for any inaccurate or repetitive information.

By law, the credit reporting agencies must remove any errors that appear on your report, but it can take 30 days or more to do so. If you know you have a financed purchase in your near future, be sure to review your report immediately so you have ample time to correct any errors before it affects your loan.

If you are in the process of purchasing a home, you will also want to monitor your report closely. Even if you have secured a mortgage commitment from the bank, you will still need to keep a watchful eye on your credit report. Banks do a last minute credit check prior to the closing. Problems with your credit report could jeopardize your home purchase, so be sure to periodically check your report until you close on your new home.

Even if you do not plan to make any major purchases, checking your report periodically can alert you to any issues or potential identity theft. It is a good policy to review your report quarterly to ensure that your finances are on the right track.

When applying for mortgage financing, your credit score is going to be one of the first things a potential lender looks at. Especially these days when lenders are tightening lending requirements; a good score can be especially important.

Credit scores are used by mortgage lenders to determine your level of financial responsibility. A low credit score may indicate that you might be a bad credit risk, which could mean that you might default on your mortgage loan.

Of course, other factors are also taken into consideration when applying for a mortgage loan, such as a person's income and employment status. However, the credit score can often be the deciding factor. Even if you are approved for a mortgage loan with less than perfect credit, there will be a price to be paid. This is because only individuals who have good credit ratings will qualify for the best interest rates.

Chapter 9

REASONS FOR EXCELLENT CREDIT

The person who doesn't know where his next dollar is coming from usually doesn't know where his last dollar went."

--Unknown

When the use of a thing is unknown, abuse is inevitable. These are not my words, but an adage which saves a man in a quest to live a good life.

The reason why many fail to achieve their financial goals is their inability to manage their credit. In America, a good credit score can be a financial tool you can use to leverage the playing field in our capitalistic society. Research reveals that an average credit score in the US is at an all-time high of 695; though this varies in terms of the model, age, population, states, income levels, and other factors. Meanwhile, a score of 720 and above is tagged excellent and less than 660 is regarded as a poor credit score. In this chapter, I will be listing the major importance of why you need good credit in America.

Some people wonder if they really need to keep good credit. Many financial experts will tell you that credit doesn't matter if you plan to be out of debt, because you won't be borrowing money going forward, so what does your credit matter?

There are three elements of money that eat away the principle; they are taxes, interest, and insurance. These three elements make up the majority of where our money goes throughout our lifetime. It's true that most people in the working class will make over a million dollars in their lifetime, but the question remains: How can you retain most of what you've earned? My suggestion is, get a good CPA or tax advisor, make it a habit of shopping for insurance and invest in getting those credit scores above 750.

Ideally speaking, it would be great to get the best interest rates for those major purchases, and having excellent credit will definitely cut the expenses over a long period of time. Here are a few things to consider as you make those major purchases. When you think of excellent FICO scores, think of how much money you will save.

•Buying A House

Someday, especially if you are young, you will want to buy a place of your own, and that will require some high standards when it comes to credit and your credit score. Most lenders require a minimum credit score of 680 to qualify for a fixed rate mortgage.

You always want to shoot for a fixed rate as it limits your monthly payment to a fixed amount, so there are no surprises down the road. If you choose a 30-year fixed rate, keep your options open to paying it like a 15-year mortgage due to the fact that the interest on a 30-year mortgage will have a compound effect.

Take the time to go over your amortization schedule so you can clearly see how your interest payments are calculated against the principal payments.

• Financing A Car

Similar to buying a house, you will need a good credit score to finance the purchase of your next vehicle. Most banks and even car dealers will offer you a better rate if your credit score is higher. And obviously, we all want the lowest rate when borrowing money.

My suggestion for financing any type of highly depreciating asset like a car is to borrow only up to 60-70 percent on the car's loan value. This provides you with an equity safety net which will help you get a jump start on paying the loan off before the value of the car can drop too much.

Note: If you plan on purchasing a home DO NOT finance a vehicle until you have gone over the numbers on what your debt to income ratio would be if you purchased a home.

• Getting A Job

Like it or not, many employers have began running credit checks on their candidates. In fact, 47 percent of employers admitted to running your credit when you apply for a job. After all, if you're being hired to work for someone, they want to know how responsible you are with your own money. This is a good indicator that your employer cares about habits including: can you manage your responsibilities, are you timely and are you an integrity-laden person?

At this time there is no data suggesting that employers are using FICO scores as a factor in their decision-making process.

• Starting A Business

Every year, thousands of Americans decide to start their own business. However, getting a business up and running isn't always easy and usually takes some significant funding to get going and stay afloat.

Depending on the type of business you want to start, you may need to have your local community bank to help you make your dreams a reality and succeed. Even if you plan to borrow money in your business' name, most banks require a credit check and evaluation of the partners of the business; because after all, you are the one who will be making the decisions.

• **Emergencies**

Dave Ramsey always says that many times in life, "Murphy shows up at your door and wants to stay awhile." He is referring to the concept of Murphy's Law. The infamous statement that, "If something can go wrong, it will go wrong."

We all find ourselves in this situation at some point in our lives when things just seem to happen for the worst. Your car breaks down two weeks from payday, your furnace goes out in the middle of winter - or worse, you lose your job. Now what? Our philosophy for all our readers is that we encourage living debt free as much as possible, but sometimes you just have to borrow some money to make things work.

• Insurance

Car insurance companies are another group that have adopted the use of credit scores to help determine risk. Studies have shown that drivers with low credit scores are more likely to file insurance claims. And since claims cost the insurance companies money, they want to make sure that the people more apt to file them are charged accordingly. For this reason, the vast majority of auto insurance companies factor in your score when drawing up a policy. The lower your score is, the more you will have to pay in insurance premiums.

Credit card companies also take your credit score into account, which is something most people were aware of, but not everyone realizes the extent of. Since a credit card is similar to a loan, in that you are granted a line of credit that you are required to pay back with interest, it makes sense that credit card companies factor your score into how much credit you can get approved for and at what interest rate. What many fail to realize is that these figures are not fixed. A credit card company likes to include a "universal default" provision in their contracts in which they reserve the right to monitor your credit reports and increase the credit card interest rate if you have late payments or other negative items added to your credit reports, even if they are completely unrelated to the credit card account.

Since credit card debt is unsecured and can be dismissed in a bankruptcy, credit card companies work hard to make sure that if your finances get out of control, they are going to collect as much money from you as possible. Any indication that you might be having trouble making payments and they may start working to offset any future losses.

As you can see, a good credit score opens up a world of opportunities and has benefits many people didn't even realize were there. On the flip side, a bad credit score can be a huge roadblock causing people to have to work much harder in just about every facet of their finances.

Chapter **10**

IT'S TOO EXPENSIVE TO BE POOR IN AMERICA

"It's good to have money and the things that money can buy, but it's good, too, to check up once in a while and make sure that you haven't lost the things that money can't buy."

--George Lorimer

These were the words uttered by 2016 Presidential Candidate Bernie Sanders. In a sense, what Sanders meant by this was that the upper class are left with a lot of spare cash to invest in their future. They engage in many cost-saving activities that reduce the cost of living in the long run.

To understand Sanders' statement about the poor more clearly, every class of individual spends the same proportion on housing, clothing, and entertainment. The major difference comes when we observe the rich's spending on education and retirement savings.

According to Sanders, the average cost of living, or feeding, to be specific, of the average poor person is significantly higher by virtue of their purchasing habits.

Sanders made quite strong points that are justified by facts and data found in various studies. Poor people, due to the fact that they don't have enough money on-hand, incur more cost. They frequent the retailers for their daily basic necessities. These retailers make a profit off of them as they buy in small quantities, unlike the rich that purchase in bulk and enjoy the incurred discounts.

Renting is common among the poor, as they can't afford to own a home. Calculating their total spending over a long period will convince you of how they are living more expensively than the rich. The amount they must have used to secure their housing over a period of time could have been utilized to own it. This is a benefit the rich enjoy, and a fact which Sanders pointed out in his speech. The poor are burdened by the interest rates they are made to pay adding to their cost of living. While on the other hand, the rich enjoy interest rates on their saving.

Although Sanders was intermixing absolute poverty and relative poverty, he was really nailing it. While absolute poverty is that there are minimum standards below which no one anywhere in the world should ever fall, what he had in mind was actually relative poverty in Baltimore, where some have more than others in the society. Bad credit makes life even more expensive. Just imagine barely qualifying for a loan and paying the highest rates available. It's very difficult to build wealth when most of your money is going to interest.

Most consumers believe this idea that having a fixed rate mortgage is the most cost-effective way to go. However, the fixed rate, over a 30-year period, compounds, causing this kind of loan to be very expensive, especially if you were to couple that with a subprime interest rate.

Surely homeownership remains an important goal for most Americans. Most renters hope to become homeowners once they have good credit and can muster the necessary financial resources to handle the responsibilities that come with owning a home.

A lot of financial benefits abound in homeownership; one of the major factors is tax savings. For most Americans, there are tax savings associated with owning a home. Price appreciation, which helps build home equity, is another incentive. In all, we can unanimously agree to the fact that renting can be chosen as a result of income constraints. Yet, as a means of building wealth, however, there is no practical substitute for homeownership.

Low credit scores can be a core relation to low income as well. When consumers depend on credit as a lifestyle, that can be an indication of poor financial health. If you are missing payments, over-utilizing your available credit and/or constantly applying for new credit, it may be an indication of a severe lack of cash flow. I believe our school system should invest more in financial literacy as a way to prepare students for the real world. I also believe there are certain life lessons that can only be taught through real-life experiences.

As a student of money, myself, I understand that handling money and creating a budget is a mindset as well as a skill set. It's perfectly okay to fail when you are learning a skill, and handling money is a skill! It takes practice to handle an ever-changing budget. My budget when I was single was drastically different from the one I have with a wife and three kids. I assume it's the same for you as well. My advice is: write it down and track your progress.

I hope by now you have an understanding of how credit scores work and how much they govern the circular flow of money. It is no secret that debt is a driver of our economy.

On the flip side, what would happen if no one had access to capital? There are greater things that may outweigh the cost of interest on a loan, one being "opportunity cost."

Think of the many countries in this world where banks are not available, and people don't have access to lending institutions. We call them third world countries. So, while some may frown on debt altogether, truth be told, America was built on a loan. Where would the American dream be without the ability to finance that dream?

Chapter 11

CREDIT REPORTING

"Chase the vision, not the money; the money will end up following you."

--Tony Hsieh, CEO of Zappos

The purpose of FICO scores is for lending institutions to have an idea of how much risk they may assume when granting consumers credit. This is why it is imperative that you attempt to maintain an impeccable credit profile.

This book is not about credit repair or disputing negative items but taking preventative actions to ensure good credit. My goal was to lay out a clear distinction of the FICO score apart from the credit reporting and the credit repair industry. Also, to make sure you have practical applications for the use of the industry-specific FICO scoring models.

As consumers, we often believe that credit reporting and credit scoring are synonymous, but in fact, they are two systems working together. Good credit scores depend on accurate credit reporting. Accurate credit reporting depends on accurate data. We can't expect maximum scores if the data being reported is flawed and the way it is reported has an adverse effect on our scores.

There are two things to keep in mind:

1. Your responsibility as a consumer is to take control of your credit.

2. The credit bureaus and data furnishers are responsible for getting it right the first time. Be accountable and hold them accountable.

The next book in the works will deal with credit reporting and credit repair in more detail. For now, I do want to address the credit reporting agencies AKA the big three.

Even if you've been perfectly responsible with handling credit, there is still a severe problem with how consumer data is being reported through the credit bureaus. How common is it for the credit bureaus to report erroneously? You would be shocked if I told you the scores are different across the board because the data does not match accurately. The credit reporting agencies report data to their customers. Who are their customers? Companies that buy data, such as marketing agencies, banks, employers, insurance companies, etc.

What is most commonly overlooked is credit optimization. If, in fact, you do have positive credit, it is important to make sure that the positive accounts are reporting properly across all three credit bureaus. When most consumers read a report, they only look for the derogatory items. However, a credit card with positive information not reporting to all three credit bureaus could be just as harmful as a charge-off. Remember, no credit is worse than bad credit.

There are potential data points that can be either inaccurate or not fully reported on an account. It's best to review all three credit bureaus side-by-side. This way you get an idea of where the errors are. When I check a report with different dates, balances, account types, etc, we must conclude that if the data points are different, they cannot all be accurate. For example, either the account was opened on May 1st or May 31st, but it can't be both.

You see, the point is this, if a creditor has sent in information about a particular account, there is no way those data points should show up on a credit report with different information. There should be consistency on each credit report from all three credit bureaus.

Another major issue is when credit bureaus find errors there is no reasonable investigation. It's simple, they automate the dispute process altogether. Meaning all disputes go through the E-oscar or OCR system. It's computer data being verified by a computer.

Here is another problem that's common, medical debt. Medical debt is the most common item that appears on a credit report and the number one reason people file for bankruptcy. Really, there is no true test that proves the consumer was irresponsible for not paying a bill. It could simply be a miscommunication from the consumer's health insurance provider. This same consumer could be suffering from low scores, just like someone who mishandled a few credit cards. No one cares why your credit is bad in the marketplace. Lenders are not in the compassion business, they only look at the numbers.

Since we understand that it's common for the credit bureaus to get it wrong, the key is to look at the credit report for missing, incomplete and/or inaccurate information. We will go into further detail in my next book, The Good Credit Revolution! Stay tuned in!

If you are a person who has done his or her best to pay your bills on time, live within your means, and use credit responsibly, you already know the value of maintaining good credit. You also know that having a good credit rating is a powerful, positive force in your life. If however, you are a person who has struggled to manage your money, or if your credit accounts are over-extended, you may need some help to restore and maintain a good credit rating. Fortunately, there are steps you can take to properly manage your credit.

There are too many variables in our lives to control everything, but we can control what we are responsible for. Making and sticking to a budget, paying bills on time, and using credit responsibly are steps you can take to improve your financial life. Maintaining good credit is hard work, but it is work that always bears good fruit.

We should always strive to build our cash reserve and increase our cash flow. This will always be the top priority and the only way to do so is to stick to a plan. Life will always throw curve balls at us, but not preparing is just like waiting to strike out.

We must not only change what we think and how we feel about money but also be a voice of change in the midst of our community. Culture is powerful because there is a system at work that no one has to talk about, but everyone knows it's there. If we were to counter the culture, our behavior must be the catalyst for this change.

Acknowledgments

I would like to thank my lovely wife Rhonda for all of her support from day one. I also want to thank our three beautiful kids, Laniah, Lawrence Jr. and Isaiah for being the best kids on earth. To my family and friends who have always supported my vision to help educate and empower those in our community.

Thank you all !

Follow me online:

www.lawrencedmartin.com

www.facebook.com/officialLawrenceMartin

https://www.instagram.com/official_Lawrence_M artin

https://www.linkedin.com/in/lawrence-martin-99031143/